I0816575

SEE-GULLS OCEAN TOURS

DISCOVERING MARINE REPTILES

by Charis Mather

Fusion Books, an imprint of Bearport Publishing by FlutterBee

Credits
All images are courtesy of Shutterstock.com, unless otherwise stated. Recurring – Net Vector, Baskiabat, NotionPic, PCH.Vector, Susann Guenther, LAtelier. Cover – Danny Ye, Efrus, Shane Myers Photography. 2–3 – Michael Smith ITWP. 4–5 – MVshop, Damsea. 6–7 – ako photography, Roberto La Rosa. 8–9 – Bradley Olson, WaterAndMagic. 10–11 – Lauren Suryanata. 12–13 – DiveIvanov, Tracy Immordino. 14–15 – Jack Pokoj, Rich Carey. 16–17 – Tartila, Maridav, MDay Photography. 18–19 – wildestanimal, Julio Salgado. 20–21 – Ken Griffiths, John Fader. 22–23 – Evannovostro, Tetsuo Arada.

Bearport Publishing Company Product Development Team
Kayla Eggert, Theresa Emminizer, Kim Jones, Allison Juda, Cole Nelson, Naomi Reich, Steve Scheluchin, Tiana Tran

Library of Congress Cataloging-in-Publication Data is available at www.loc.gov or upon request from the publisher.

ISBN: 979-8-89577-813-5 (hardcover)
ISBN: 979-8-89577-825-8 (ebook)

For more information, write to Bearport Publishing, 3500 American Blvd W, Suite 150, Bloomington, MN 55431.
Printed in the United States of America.

CONTENTS

ALL ABOARD!

Ahoy there! You are just in time for the See-Gulls Ocean Tour. I am Captain Gulliver, and this is my **crew**. Today, we are looking out for marine reptiles.

All marine reptiles live at sea, but some live further out than others. Most marine reptiles come to land from time to time as well.

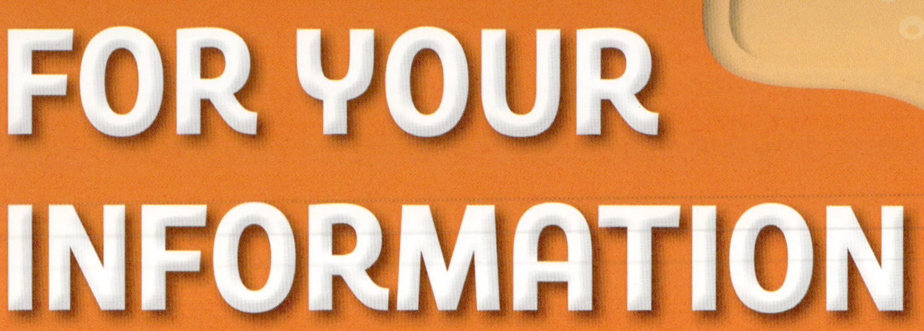

FOR YOUR INFORMATION

Reptiles are animals that breathe air and are cold-blooded. This means that their body **temperatures** change with the temperatures around them.

Most reptiles live on land. Marine reptiles have special **adaptations** that help them live in the ocean. Most are very good swimmers and can hold their breath for a long time.

Many marine reptiles have salt glands. These special body parts help them live in salty sea water.

LOGGERHEAD TURTLES

Loggerhead turtles can hold their breaths for up to seven hours when resting! They sleep at the bottom of the sea and come up for air when they wake up.

Loggerheads also hold their breaths for a long time while diving for food.

When loggerhead turtles are ready to have young, they come to land. They lay eggs in the sand. As soon as the eggs hatch, the baby turtles head for the sea.

SALTWATER CROCODILES

Saltwater crocodiles can grow to be 23 feet (7 m) long! They often hide their big bodies under the water so that only their eyes peek out.

Saltwater crocodiles have one of the strongest bites in the world!

When an animal comes near, saltwater crocodiles jump out to attack! They snap up **prey** in their strong jaws.

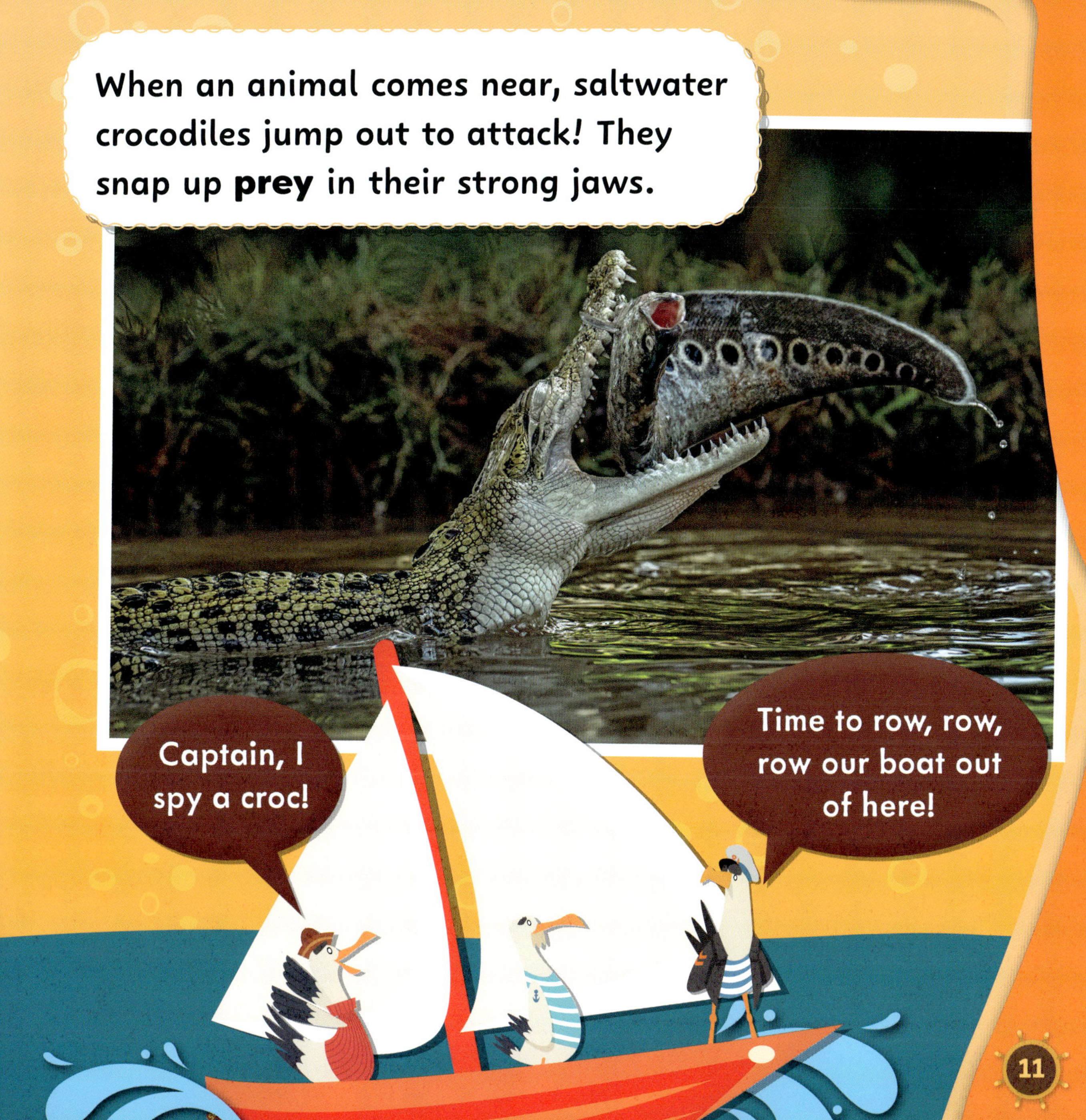

GREEN SEA TURTLES

Green sea turtles get their color from the green seagrasses and **algae** that they eat.

SEAGRASS

These turtles can often be seen lying around on the shore in big groups. They do this to warm up in the sun.

Green sea turtles are the only turtles that regularly sun themselves on land.

BANDED SEA KRAITS

The **coral reef** is the perfect place to find banded sea kraits. Their long, stripy bodies are thin enough to move through gaps in the coral as the snakes look for prey.

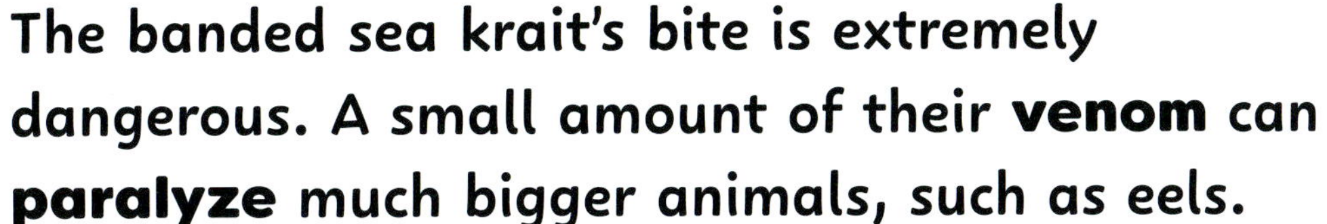

The banded sea krait's bite is extremely dangerous. A small amount of their **venom** can **paralyze** much bigger animals, such as eels.

These snakes can spend up to 30 minutes underwater before they need to come up for air.

Try not to look tasty!

MARINE IGUANAS

Marine iguanas are the only lizards on Earth that eat in the ocean! They sun themselves on rocky shores and dive into the water to look for food.

Marine iguanas can be found only around the Galápagos Islands.

Since the sea is very salty, marine iguanas get more salt than their bodies need. To get rid of the extra salt, the reptiles spray it out through their noses with a powerful sneeze.
Bless you!

LEATHERBACK TURTLES

Instead of a hard shell, leatherback turtles have soft, rubbery skin on their backs. These turtles start out small, but they grow to be the biggest of all turtles.

A BABY LEATHERBACK TURTLE

The leatherback's soft shell makes it possible for this turtle to dive much deeper than other turtles. They can swim down 4,000 ft. (1,200 m) below the surface and hold their breaths for up to 85 minutes!
Leatherback turtles hunt jellyfish deep in the sea.

YELLOW-BELLIED SEA SNAKES

Careful! These sea snakes are venomous.

Yellow-bellied sea snakes spend most of their time in the open waters. They even have babies in the water.

To stay healthy, yellow-bellied sea snakes shed their skin often. Most snakes do this by rubbing against the ground. But yellow-bellied sea snakes shed by tying themselves in knots and rubbing against their own bodies.

Shedding is replacing old skin with new skin.

BACK ON LAND!

Well, that was exciting! All of these marine reptiles have been very interesting, but it's time to get back on dry land.

We hope you will join us on another See-Gulls Ocean Tour soon. There is always more to explore in the ocean.
See-*gull* you next time!

GLOSSARY

adaptations changes to animals that help them live better in their environments

algae plantlike living things that are usually found in water

coral reef rocklike structures formed from the skeletons of sea animals called polyps

crew the group of people who work on a ship

paralyze to cause a body part to stop being able to move, which often comes with a loss of feeling

prey animals that are hunted by other animals for food

temperatures how hot or cold things are

venom a harmful substance that is injected through a bite or a sting

INDEX